I0763562

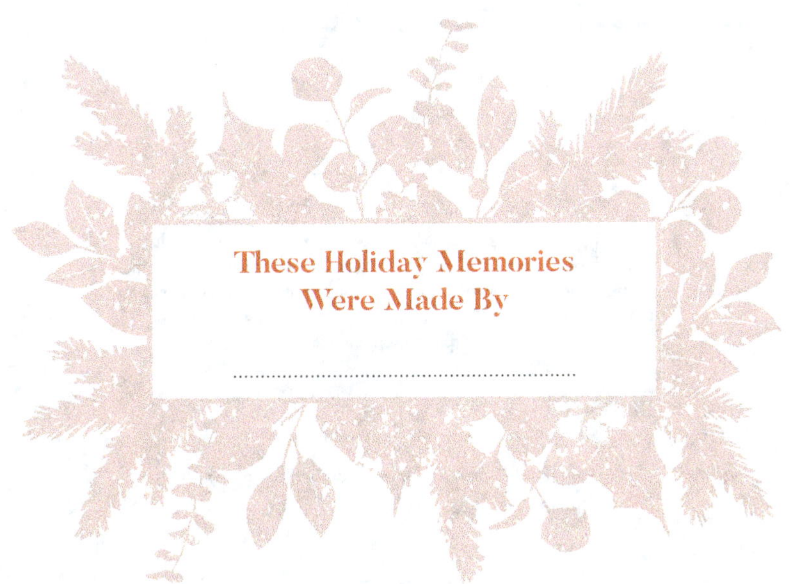

These Holiday Memories
Were Made By

....

This book was a gift from

....

Front cover/book design by VisualPhilosophy.

ISBN: 978-1629672656

Library of Congress Control Number: 2023919073

Published by Wise Media Group, Morro Bay, California

Created by Rip Gerber

Visit www.ripgerber.com to learn more
of the inspiration behind *Holiday Memories*

Holiday Memories

Holiday Memories is a decade-long journal designed to safeguard your cherished moments. It offers ample room for jotting thoughts, preserving important notes, and storing pictures. This ensures you always remember the precious times spent with loved ones.

The holidays are a special time of the year to celebrate, give thanks, help each other, and embrace new beginnings. Christmas time, while celebrated in our own unique way, brings us together in a spirit of sharing, community, love, and wonder.

The Holiday Memories journal is designed to help you capture these moments and share your holiday journey with future generations. With space for cards and pictures, we've designed it to capture 10 years of personalized holiday memories. Use this journal to capture the memories you want to keep and it'll become a personalized book you and your loved ones will cherish year after year.

Inspiration & Dedication

Since pagan times, men and women all over the world have celebrated the arrival of Winter and the coming of Spring by lighting fires and feasting. Many elements of these early pagan rituals, stories and customs contributed to the ways we celebrate the holiday season today.

In ancient Roman times, the Winter Solstice festival called Saturnalia honored the god of agriculture Saturn, with December 25th celebrated as the birth of Mithra, their sun god. Centuries later, as Christianity spread through Europe, the clergy adopted many of the local pagan customs into the celebration of the birth of Jesus.

In 350 AD, Pope Julius I, the bishop of Rome, proclaimed December 25 the official celebration day for Jesus' birthday. The Germans called the celebration jōl, which referred to the feast of the winter solstice and later became 'Yule.' Other Europeans referred to the celebration in their own ways: Navidad (Spanish), Natale (Italian) and Noël (French). The English termed the festival Christmas, meaning "mass on Christ's day." Today, the term Christmas is known worldwide.

Traditions of the Winter Solstice and of Christmastime vary by country, culture, and region, yet all share common traits of celebration, gratitude, giving, welcoming the new, the gathering of families and friends, and wishes of love and good fortune ahead. Some of the ways Christmas is celebrated around the globe are surprising – some may even seem odd – yet they all share in a fellowship of sharing, community, love and wonder.

Your own celebrations through the years create and reinforce your personal traditions that will remain with you and your loved ones for years. This Holiday Memories journal is for you, to help you capture those moments of the season each and every year, so that you may enjoy the past celebrations and share your holiday journeys with generations to come.

In the spirit of giving and of Christmas, the author of Holiday Memories has donated proceeds from the sale of this book to The Guardsmen. The Guardsmen makes a life-changing difference in the lives of at-risk youth by raising funds for scholarships, campership, and other youth programs. Each year The Guardsmen sends 2,500 at-risk youth to outdoor education programs and provides scholarship support to more than 250 students in need. Learn more at: www.guardsmen.org.

Happy Holidays! RIP GERBER

Holiday Memories

Place your holiday card or picture here

Where we spent the holidays

What the weather was like

What was happening in the world

What filled us with holiday spirit this year

Place a picture of
your Christmas tree here

A favorite tradition celebrated

Thanksgiving

Decorating memories

Christmas Eve

Christmas Day

Favorite gifts

Favorite foods and meals

• YULE GOAT •

(SWEDEN)

The Yule Goat honors the mythical Norse goats that pulled the god Thor's chariot. The Yule Goat first appeared alongside Saint Nicholas in 11th century pagan celebrations for its power to control the devil. By the 17th century, young men in Sweden would dress up as the goat creature and pull pranks, but in the 19th century, the Yule Goat became a symbol of good: fathers would dress up as the Yule Goat and hand out family gifts. In 1966, the ancient Swedish Christmas symbol was reimagined as a giant straw goat in red ribbons known as Gävle Goat. Every December a 42-foot-tall straw goat is constructed at Gävle's Castle Square.

Favorite movies and books this year

Favorite songs this year

AUSTRALIA

Christmastime is summertime in Australia, which means surfing. Down under, Santa Claus arrives by surfboard instead of a sleigh.

Memorable trips, parties, and events

Place the favorite greeting card you received here

One moment we will always treasure

Special acts of kindess

Special visitors we welcomed

The New Year

• HOLIDAY SONGS •

Many people ring in the holidays with carols and holiday hits. Which of these Top 100 holiday songs are your holiday favorites?

Song Title	Sing Along	Enjoy Listening	Not a Favorite	Switch Off
All I Want For Christmas Is You Mariah Carey				
Rockin' Around The Christmas Tree Brenda Lee				
Jingle Bell Rock Bobby Helms				
The Christmas Song (Merry Christmas To You) Nat King Cole				
A Holly Jolly Christmas Burl Ives				
Feliz Navidad Jose Feliciano				
It's The Most Wonderful Time Of The Year Andy Williams				
Last Christmas Wham!				
Let It Snow, Let It Snow, Let It Snow Dean Martin				
White Christmas Bing Crosby				
Christmas Eve (Sarajevo 12/24) Trans-Siberian Orchestra				
Rudolph The Red-Nosed Reindeer Gene Autry				
Sleigh Ride The Ronettes				

Song Title	Sing Along	Enjoy Listening	Not a Favorite	Switch Off
It's Beginning To Look A Lot Like Christmas Michael Buble				
Mary, Did You Know? Pentatonix				
Happy Xmas (War Is Over) John & Yoko/The Plastic Ono Band				
Mistletoe Justin Bieber				
Blue Christmas Elvis Presley				
Santa Tell Me Ariana Grande				
Wonderful Christmastime Paul McCartney				
Christmas Canon Trans-Siberian Orchestra				
Underneath The Tree Kelly Clarkson				
Happy Holiday / The Holiday Season Andy Williams				
You're A Mean One, Mr. Grinch Thurl Ravenscroft				
Please Come Home For Christmas Eagles				
Hallelujah Pentatonix				
Christmastime Is Here Vince Guaraldi Trio				

Song Title	Sing Along	Enjoy Listening	Not a Favorite	Switch Off
Here Comes Santa Claus (Right Down Santa Claus Lane) Gene Autry	○	○	○	○
It's Beginning To Look A Lot Like Christmas Johnny Mathis	○	○	○	○
Santa Baby Eartha Kitt With Henri Rene And His Orchestra	○	○	○	○
Christmas (Baby Please Come Home) Darlene Love	○	○	○	○
Do They Know It's Christmas? Band Aid	○	○	○	○
It's Beginning To Look A Lot Like Christmas Perry Como And The Fontane Sisters	○	○	○	○
Linus And Lucy (Peanuts Theme) Vince Guaraldi Trio	○	○	○	○
Little Saint Nick The Beach Boys	○	○	○	○
Where Are You Christmas? Faith Hill	○	○	○	○
Run Rudolph Run Chuck Berry	○	○	○	○
It's Beginning To Look A Lot Like Christmas Bing Crosby With Jud Conlon's Rhythmaires	○	○	○	○
Jingle Bells Frank Sinatra	○	○	○	○
(There's No Place Like) Home For The Holidays (1959) Perry Como With Mitchell Ayers	○	○	○	○
Santa Claus Is Comin' To Town Bruce Springsteen	○	○	○	○
Santa Claus Is Comin' To Town Jackson 5	○	○	○	○
Little Drummer Boy Pentatonix	○	○	○	○
Holly Jolly Christmas Michael Buble	○	○	○	○
Christmas (Baby Please Come Home) Mariah Carey	○	○	○	○
Frosty The Snowman Jimmy Durante	○	○	○	○

Song Title	Sing Along	Enjoy Listening	Not a Favorite	Switch Off
Have Yourself A Merry Little Christmas Frank Sinatra	○	○	○	○
Have Yourself A Merry Little Christmas Michael Buble	○	○	○	○
This Christmas Donny Hathaway	○	○	○	○
Do You Want To Build A Snowman? Kristen Bell, Agatha Lee Monn & Katie Lopez	○	○	○	○
Merry Christmas Darling Carpenters	○	○	○	○
All I Want For Christmas Is You Michael Buble	○	○	○	○
Sleigh Ride Leroy Anderson	○	○	○	○
Rudolph The Red-Nosed Reindeer Burl Ives	○	○	○	○
Here Comes Santa Claus (Right Down Santa Claus Lane) Elvis Presley	○	○	○	○
Baby It's Cold Outside Dean Martin	○	○	○	○
Let It Snow, Let It Snow, Let It Snow Frank Sinatra With The B. Swanson Quartet	○	○	○	○
Last Christmas Taylor Swift	○	○	○	○
I Want A Hippopotamus For Christmas Gayla Peevey	○	○	○	○
The Little Drummer Boy The Harry Simeone Chorale	○	○	○	○
Baby It's Cold Outside Idina Menzel Duet With Michael Buble	○	○	○	○
White Christmas The Drifters Featuring Clyde McPhatter And Bill Pinkney	○	○	○	○
Deck The Halls Nat King Cole	○	○	○	○
Merry Christmas, Happy Holidays 'N Sync	○	○	○	○
I Saw Mommy Kissing Santa Claus Jackson 5	○	○	○	○
O Tannenbaum Vince Guaraldi Trio	○	○	○	○

Song Title	Sing Along	Enjoy Listening	Not a Favorite	Switch Off
Jingle Bell Rock Daryl Hall John Oates				
Christmas (Baby Please Come Home) Michael Buble				
White Christmas Michael Buble Duet With Shania Twain				
Like It's Christmas Jonas Brothers				
Mele Kalikimaka (Merry Christmas) Bing Crosby & The Andrews Sisters				
The Chipmunk Song (Christmas Don't Be Late) David Seville & The Chipmunks				
Silent Night The Temptations				
I'll Be Home For Christmas Bing Crosby				
O Come All Ye Faithful Nat King Cole				
What Christmas Means To Me John Legend Featuring Stevie Wonder				
That's Christmas To Me Pentatonix				
Santa Claus Is Coming To Town Michael Buble				
Cozy Little Christmas Katy Perry				
Winter Wonderland Darlene Love				
Carol Of The Bells David Foster				
Have Yourself A Merry Little Christmas Sam Smith				
You Make It Feel Like Christmas Gwen Stefani Featuring Blake Shelton				
I'll Be Home For Christmas Michael Buble				

Song Title	Sing Along	Enjoy Listening	Not a Favorite	Switch Off
Do You Hear What I Hear? Whitney Houston				
The Christmas Shoes NewSong				
Do You Hear What I Hear? Bing Crosby With Ralph Carmichael Orchestra				
Carol Of The Bells John Williams				
All I Want For Christmas Is You Vince Vance & The Valiants				
Silver Bells Andy Williams				
Do You Hear What I Hear? Andy Williams				
Home For The Holidays Carpenters				
Mary Did You Know Jordan Smith				
This Christmas Chris Brown				
What Christmas Means To Me Stevie Wonder				
O Holy Night Josh Groban				
Christmas In Hollis Run-D.M.C.				
Winter Wonderland / Don't Worry Be Happy Pentatonix Featuring Tori Kelly				
Jingle Bells Michael Buble Featuring The Puppini Sisters				
White Winter Hymnal Pentatonix				

Holiday Memories

Place your holiday card or picture here

Where we spent the holidays

What the weather was like

What was happening in the world

What filled us with holiday spirit this year

Place a picture of
your Christmas tree here

A favorite tradition celebrated

Thanksgiving

Decorating memories

Christmas Eve

Christmas Day

Favorite gifts

Favorite foods and meals

Favorite songs this year

SLOVAKIA

A spoonful of Christmas kutya, a pudding made of cooked wheat mixed with honey and nuts, is thrown at the ceiling: if it sticks it means good fortune in the new year.

• LA NOCHE • DE RÁBANOS

(MEXICO)

On December 23, hundreds of professional food artisans and residents of Oaxaca, Mexico, compete in the Noche de Rábanos, or Night of the Radishes, in which participants carve Nativity scenes, Mexican folklore and holiday images into the skin of large radishes. The ancient festival was started by local merchants to draw shoppers to the town plaza. The three-day festival is considered the most impressive display of carved vegetables in the world.

Memorable trips, parties, and events

Favorite movies and books this year

Place the favorite greeting card you received here

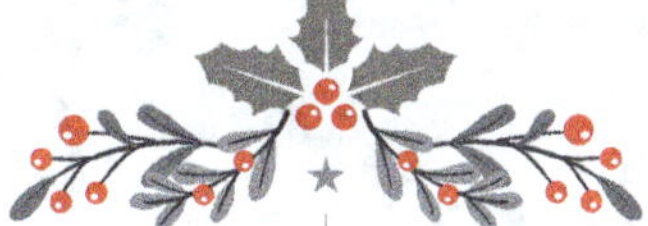

One moment we will always treasure

Special acts of kindess

Special visitors we welcomed

The New Year

• CELEBRATIONS •
AROUND THE WORLD

November

HANNUKAH
Hanukkah changes dates every year and provides eight days to celebrate with small gifts, candle lighting, and special Hannukkah-inspired treats.

THANKSGIVING
Primarily celebrated in the United States, this holiday originated as a fall harvest feast between the Pilgrims and the Native Americans.

December

3rd
KRAMPUSNACHT
In Austria, the evil accomplice of Saint Nicholas begins to roam the streets frightening children and punishing the bad.

3rd
JULEBORD
In Norway, Christmas begins on December 3 with the hiding of brooms and mops to prevent witches and other mischievous spirits from returning on Christmas Eve to steal the cleaning sticks and fly through the skies.

4th
NATIONAL COOKIE DAY
Created in 1987 by the Blue Chip Cookie Company based out of San Francisco.

5th
ST. NICHOLAS EVE
In Europe, this evening celebration honors St. Nicholas, the patron saint of Christmas, gift giving, and children.

6th
LA QUEMA DEL DIABLO
In Guatemala, this day marks 'the Burning of the Devil.' Families construct effigies of Satan and build bonfires outside their homes and burn them.

6th
SINTERKLAAS DAY
Also known as St. Nicholas Day in Europe, this is usually a day where small gifts or stockings full of candy and treats are given out.

8th
BODHI DAY
Celebrated in Japan (and in China as 'The Laba Festival') this day honors the enlightenment of Siddhartha Gautama.

8th
FEAST OF THE IMMACULATE CONCEPTION
The Feast of the Immaculate Conception is a day to pay tribute to the Blessed Virgin Mary around the world.

12th
JÓLASVEINA
The Yuletide Lads visit Icelandic homes from December 12-24. The lads are mischievous and originally were supposed to scare naughty children.

13th
ST. LUCIA DAY
Sweden celebrates St. Lucia Day on December 13, when children wear white, carry candles, and provide sweet treats for their family members.

16th
LAS POSADAS
The start of a nine-day Latin American celebration commemorating the journey of Joseph and Mary from Nazareth to Bethlehem and their search for lodgings.

21st
YULE
Winter Solstice is the shortest day of the year and has been celebrated in countries around the world since the 4th century. This midwinter festival lasts for twelve days, beginning on the Winter Solstice.

22nd

'EL GORDO.'

The Spanish National Lottery holds the country's biggest lottery of the year called 'El Gordo' or 'The Fat One.' The winning numbers are sung by a choir of twenty-two school children.

23rd

LA NOCHE DE RÁBANOS

In Mexico, hundreds of professional food artisans and residents of Oaxaca, Mexico, compete in the 'Night of the Radishes,' in which participants carve Nativity scenes, Mexican folklore and holiday images into the skin of large radishes.

23rd

LITTLE CHRISTMAS EVE

Norway's "little Christmas Eve" takes place on the 23rd, a time to gather with just your immediate family and do something fun like craft gingerbread houses.

25th

CHRISTMAS DAY

Over 2 billion people (over a third of the world's population) celebrate the birth of Christ.

26th

ST. STEPHEN'S DAY

Acknowledges when St. Stephen was killed by stones after preaching to his people for 40 days.

26th

KWANZAA

Kwanzaa is a seven-day celebration, which stretches from December 26 through the new year, where families light candles each night and exchange handmade gifts.

26th

BOXING DAY

Originating in the United Kingdom in the Middle Ages when servants were required to work on Christmas. The day after they could visit their families, and employers gave each servant a box containing gifts and bonuses.

26th

JUNKANOO

In the Bahamas and throughout the Caribbean, festivals are held Boxing Day, December 26 and again on New Year's Day. Dating back to its African heritage choreographed dancers sing and and perform in traditional handmade colorful costumes.

31st

SILVESTER-CHLAUSEN

Celebrated in Appenzell, Switzerland, dating back to the 15th century, it's part of Saint Sylvester's Day and New Year's Mummer tradition.

31st

HOGMANAY

The "Moon of the Hag," is celebrated in Scotland as the last day of the year with gift-giving and visiting with friends and neighbors.

31st

ŌMISOKA

Considered the second-most important day in Japan, families gather for one last time in the old year to have a bowl of toshikoshi-soba.

January

5th

LA BEFANA

In Italy, a kind witch flies around on the eve of the Epiphany to deliver toys to children.

6th

THREE KINGS DAY

In countries such as Venezuela and the Philippines, January 6 is the day of the Reyes Magos (Three Kings) with celebration, gifts and feasting.

6th

ARMENIAN CHRISTMAS

In regions outside the influence of the Roman Empire, such as Armenia, January 6 is considered the official date of the birth of Christ.

7th

ORTHODOX CHRISTMAS

In countries including Georgia, Kazakhstan, Russia, Serbia, and the Ukraine, the Orthodox Church recognizes January 7th as the day that Jesus was born.

7th

COPTIC CHRISTMAS

Observed in Egypt and Ethiopia, the Coptic or Alexandrian calendar is used, based on the ancient Egyptian calendar.

7th

GENNA

In the Julian calendar, Christmas falls on January 7th. In Ethiopia, the holiday is called Genna, when men play a hockey-like game.

14th

MAKAR SANKRANTI

Marking the coming of spring, Makar Sankranti is observed by Hindus across India and commemorates the movement of the sun into the constellation Capricorn and honors Surya, the sun god.

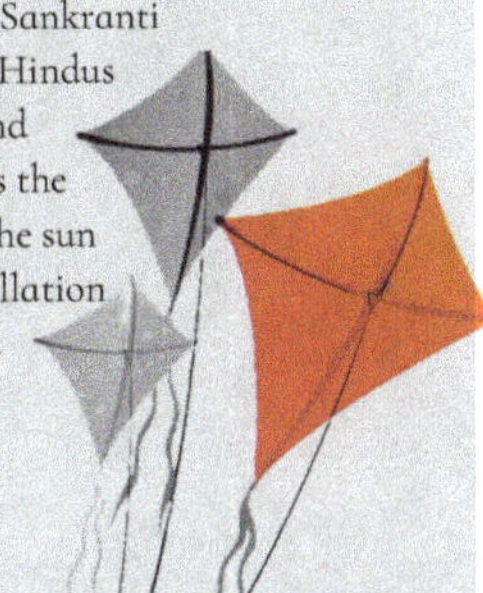

Holiday Memories

....

(YEAR)

Place your holiday card or picture here

Where we spent the holidays

What the weather was like

What was happening in the world

What filled us with holiday spirit this year

Place a picture of
your Christmas tree here

A favorite tradition celebrated

Thanksgiving

Christmas Eve

Decorating memories

Christmas Day

CANADA

Santa Claus receives mail in Canada in over 30 languages, including Braille. His address is: Santa Claus, North Pole, H0H 0H0, Canada. No stamp needed.

Favorite gifts

Favorite foods and meals

Favorite songs this year

Memorable trips, parties, and events

Favorite movies and books this year

• HIDING BROOMS •

(NORWAY)

The Christmas season in Norway is called julebord and begins December 3. According to Norwegian folklore, hiding brooms and mops prevents witches and other mischievous spirits from returning to earth on Christmas Eve to steal the cleaning sticks to fly through the skies. The pagan belief keeps the witches and wizards from interrupting Norwegian Christmas rituals including decorating the tree, making gingerbread houses, and eating *risengrynsgrøt*, a hot rice pudding.

Place the favorite greeting card you received here

One moment we will always treasure

Special acts of kindess

Special visitors we welcomed

The New Year

• HOLIDAY CHARACTERS •

Aba Chaghaloo
Afghanistan

Another name for Santa Claus in this region.

Aghios Vassilis
Greece

According to the Greek tradition, the equivalent of the Western Santa Claus in Greece is Agios Vassilis.

Badalisc
Italy

A mythical creature from the Southern Central Alps with wild glowing eyes, horns and a large mouth with sharp teeth

Babbo Natale
Italy

Known as 'Daddy Christmas,' he is Italy's version of the man in the red suit.

Christkind
Austria, Switzerland, Eastern Europe

Another name for Saint Nicholas in many countries.

Ded Moroz
Russia

'Grandfather Frost' is the Russian counterpart of Santa Claus, though Ded Moroz is much taller.

Dud Che Lao Ren
China

Santa's name in China means 'Christmas Old Man'

El Caganer
Spain

A squatting male figurine traditionally celebrated by Spanish farmers. Legend held that not including the porcelain defecating figure in a Nativity scene would bring a poor crop harvest and bad fortune.

El Niño Dios
Mexico

Translated as 'Child God,' this is Mexico's way of celebrating the baby Jesus.

Father Frost
Russia

An older man who travels with a snow maiden to deliver gifts on January 7th.

Ganesha
India

One of the most important gods in Hinduism, recognized by his elephant head and human body, this deity represents the soul (atman) and the physical (maya).

Gwiazdor
Poland

Translated as 'Star-man' for the man who brings gifts on Christmas Eve.

Hoteiosho
Japan

Although Christmas isn't widely celebrated in Japan, many Japanese celebrate this kind, gift-giving Buddhist monk named Hoteiosho.

Jólakötturinn
Iceland

The Yule Cat is a huge and vicious feline that lurks during Christmas time and eats people who have not received any new clothes to wear before Christmas Eve. Began as a legend by farmers to scare workers who didn't process their autumn wool by Christmas.

Joulupukki
Finland

Finland's Christmas figure is called Joulupukki, the Christmas goat. Also known as 'Pukki.'

Julenissen
Norway

The 'Christmas Gnome' is a short, mythological gnome-like creature with a long, white beard and a red cap, and carries a sack of toys on his back, visiting children on Christmas Eve.

Jultomten
Sweden

On Christmas Eve, the 'Christmas Elf' looks similar to Santa Claus and hides gifts for kids around their homes.

Kanakaloka
Hawaii

The Hawaiian Santa Claus often wears a Hawaiian shirt and surf shorts. His reindeer are called Leinekia, and he arrives in Hawaii in a red outrigger canoe.

Knecht Ruprecht
Germany

'Farmhand Rupert' is a devil-like character dressed in dark clothes covered with bells and a dirty beard. He travels with St. Nick and carries a stick or a small whip to punish any children who misbehave.

Krampus
Austria, Germany, and Hungary

The evil accomplice of Saint Nicholas, Krampus is a demon-like creature who frightens children and steals backs gifts.

La Befana
Italy

An old and kind witch who visits children on January 5th, the eve of the Epiphany. When the three Wise Men journeyed to greet baby Jesus, they asked Befana for directions and invited her to join them. She declined, but later regretted her decision, and now flies the skies at night like Santa and comes down the chimney to fill stockings with gifts.

Los Reyes Magos
Spain

The Three Wise Men—the bring Spanish children their gifts the night before Three Kings Day in January.

Mikulás
Hungary

Hungary's name for St. Nicholas who arrives on December 6th, St. Nicholas Day.

Papai Noel
Brazil

Papai Noel or Bom Velhinho ('Good Old Man') distributes gifts to everyone, and exchanges socks left by the window for presents.

Père Noël
France

Sometimes called 'Papa Noël' (Daddy Christmas). In France he is the legendary gift-giver at Christmas.

Santa Claus
United States

Derived from the Dutch name 'Sinterklaas', when the Coca Cola Company began its Christmas ad campaigns in the 1920, they rebranded the traditional Christmas elf into the familiar round man with white beard and red suit that we know and love today.

Saint Nikolaus
Germany and throughout Europe

Nikolaus travels by donkey on December 6 (Nikolaus Tag) and leaves coins, chocolate, oranges, and toys in the shoes of good children.

Sinterklaas
The Netherlands, Aruba, Curaçao, St. Maarten

The Dutch name for Saint Nicholas, Sinterklaas sports a long white beard, red cape, and red miter. His name is the precursor of the name Santa Claus.

Vader Kersfees
South Africa

In Afrikaan, Father Christmas (Kersvader) brings presents to the children.

Holiday Memories

Place your holiday card or picture here

Where we spent the holidays

What the weather was like

What was happening in the world

What filled us with holiday spirit this year

Place a picture of
your Christmas tree here

A favorite tradition celebrated

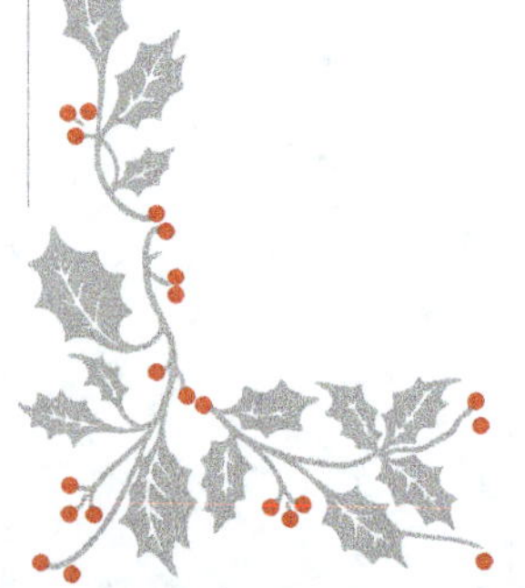

Thanksgiving

Decorating memories

Christmas Eve

Christmas Day

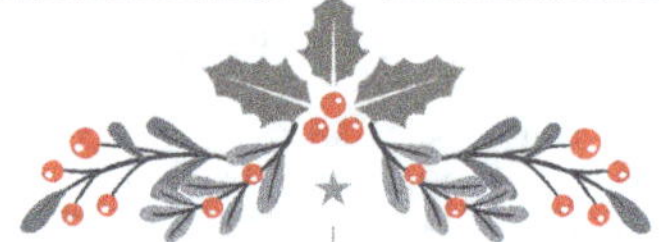

Favorite foods and meals

Favorite gifts

• POHUTUKAWA •
(NEW ZEALAND)

Down under, Christmastime falls during the summer. In place of a Christmas tree, the Kiwis celebrate with a coastal native species called the Pohutukawa that blooms red in December. The cheery crimson Pohutukawa flower is the official symbol of Christmas in New Zealand. The gnarled-root trees provide shade in the hot summer months of December and is mentioned in the local Christmas carols that Kiwis sing in both English and Maori.

Favorite songs this year

SWEDEN

Every Christmas Eve, families around Sweden gather around the television to watch the hour-long *Donald Duck Special.*

Memorable trips, parties, and events

Favorite movies and books this year

Place the favorite greeting card you received here

One moment we will always treasure

Special acts of kindess

Special visitors we welcomed

The New Year

Holiday Memories

....

(YEAR)

Place your holiday card or picture here

Where we spent the holidays

What the weather was like

What was happening in the world

What filled us with holiday spirit this year

Place a picture of
your Christmas tree here

A favorite tradition celebrated

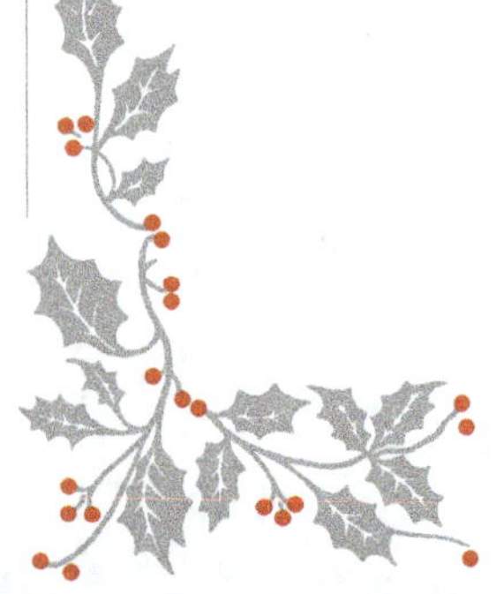

Thanksgiving

Decorating memories

Christmas Eve

Christmas Day

Favorite foods and meals

Favorite gifts

• CHRISTMAS LOG •

(SPAIN)

In the Catalonia region of Spain, gifts are delivered by the *Tió de Nadal*, the Christmas Log, a hollow piece of wood that is festooned with a smiling face, red hat and stick legs. Families blanket and 'feed' the log nightly with presents and candy starting on December 8th, the Day of the Immaculate Conception. On Christmas Eve, the log is placed in the fireplace and family members take turns bashing the log-person with a stick, commanding it to 'defecate' candies and not stinky herring, earning the log another name: *Caga Tió.* After the beating, family members reach under the log's blanket to grab the gifts.

Favorite songs this year

FINLAND

Finnish families eat a rice porridge on Christmas morning, and whoever finds the single almond placed inside one of the puddings wins a gift. At the end of Christmas day, Finnish people head for a holiday sauna.

Memorable trips, parties, and events

Favorite movies and books this year

Place the favorite greeting card you received here

One moment we will always treasure

Special acts of kindess

Special visitors we welcomed

The New Year

• HOLIDAY TREATS •

AROUND THE WORLD

Many cultures welcome the holidays in unique ways, often with food playing a central role in the celebrations. From savory feasts to sweet desserts, each culture and country brings a unique twist to cuisine during the holidays.

APPLE CIDER

Julius Caesar is said to have discovered the British drinking this tart cider in 55 BC. Europeans eventually brought the tradition of enjoying cider during the holidays to America.

BABKA

In Poland, *babka* is a traditional sweet bread dish. Polish families set out an extra serving for the lone wanderer who may pass through.

BAHN CHUNG

This rice cake – made with rice, pork, mung beans, green onions, fish sauce, and spices – is enjoyed during Tết, the Vietnamese New Year

BARSZCZ

In Poland, the holidays include a beetroot soup, a brightly-colored red broth that is usually served with small, mushroom-filled dumplings called *uszka* ('little ears').

BIBINGKA

A common holiday breakfast item in the Philippines, *bibingka* consists of rice, coconut milk, and sugar wrapped and cooked in banana leaves.

BLACK-EYED PEAS & COLLARD GREENS

Across the United States South, this dish is prepared New Year's Day to bring a year's worth of luck and financial prosperity. The meal often includes cornbread and hog jowl (the cheek of the pig).

BRAAI

Popular in South Africa, the proper way to cook *braai* is with a wooden fire while surrounded by friends and family.

BUCCELLATO

Sicilians celebrate the holidays with *buccellato*, a circular cake laced with dried figs, almonds and pine nuts. It distinctive flavor is due to marsala, a potent fortified wine.

BÛCHE DE NOËL

In France, this version of the Yule Log is a rich cake filled and rolled to look like a log and decorated with meringue-shaped mushrooms to make it look as though it were found on the forest floor.

BUTTER TARTS

Butter tarts are a Canadian dessert that's often served during Christmas. These small pastries are filled with butter, sugar, maple syrup, eggs, and sometimes walnuts and raisins.

CANDY CANES

The first candy canes from nearly 400 years ago were plain white sticks. In 1670, a German choirmaster bent the sticks to represent a shepherd's staff. In 19th century America, red stripes were added for a more festive look.

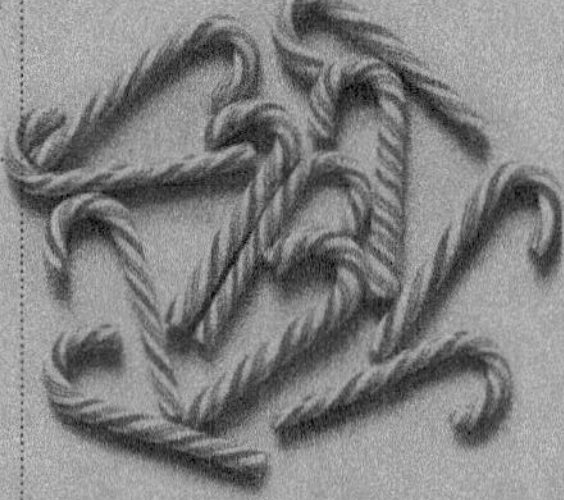

CHRISTMAS CAKE –

This British dessert, popular worldwide, is a fruit cake of flour, eggs, sugar, spices, candied cherries, dried fruit, and brandy. It's made 2 months ahead to 'feed' the cake with brandy every 2 weeks, then topped with a marzipan icing.

COAL CANDY

In Italy on the eve of Epiphany, La Befana, a broom-riding old woman delivers gifts to the good children and lumps of coal to the bad. For Italian children, the coal is often candy made with sugar, eggs and dark food coloring.

CORNED BEEF AND CABBAGE

The Irish make this dish to celebrate any special occasion but especially Christmas. Corned beef means it's salt-cured.

CURRY

In many Kwanzaa celebrations, the menu draws from the family's African traditions, which often means curries from Africa in creole dishes, or Ethiopian dishes like injera.

DUMPLINGS

Christmas is not officially celebrated in China, but Dongzhi, a Chinese festival for the Winter Solstice, includes feasting on dumplings or tangyuan, glutinous rice balls floating in sweet or savory soup.

EGGNOG

Based on the medieval drink called posset of milk, eggs, and sherry or Madeira. It was a drink for only the wealthy in Europe, until American colonists started farming the ingredients and adding rum from the Caribbean.

FAROFA

In Brazil, this breadcrumb-like mix of toasted cassava flour with butter and garlic, smoked bacon, raisins, or walnuts is often served at late Christmas Eve dinners that continue into the early hours of Christmas morning.

FEUERZANGEN BOWLE

This German mulled wine translates to 'fire tong punch' and is served in German Christmas markets. A rum-soaked sugar cone known as zuckerhut is set on fire over the wine, filling the spiced wine with drops of caramelised, boozy sugar.

FIGGY PUDDING

This cake of figs topped with brandy has been an English Christmas dessert since the mid-1600s. Itwas first banned by English Puritans because of its high alcohol content.

FISH

Many Italians partake in La Vigilia, a meat-free, seafood-heavy meal. For Italians in the United States its known as the 'Feast of the Seven Fishes.' Traditionally, Roman Catholics fast on Christmas Eve, so a feast of seven seafood dishes at the end is highly anticipated.

FRIED CHICKEN

A store manager in Tokto developed a campaign decades ago to convince the Japanese to eat Kentucky Fried Chicken for Christmas. Now, a bucket of fried chicken is a popular Christmas celebration throughout Japan, often enjoyed with cake and champagne.

FRIED PLANTAINS

In many Central and South American countries, holiday festivities often include fried plantains

FRUIT CAKE

The fruitcake was developed in Egypt, with many variations now served over the globe during the holidays.

GINGERBREAD

The first-known recipe is from Greece in 2400 BC, but became a Christmas tradition in England under Queen Elizabeth, who used it to make and decorate cookies during the holidays.

GLÜHWEIN

Also called mulled wine, this sweetened, spiced red wine is popular in Europe during the holidays.

GRAPES

In Spain, New Year's Eve revelers eat 12 green grapes at midnight, one for each month. All 12 must be consumed by the last chime to assure good luck for the year.

HANGIKJÖT

A popular Icelandic holiday foods that means "hung meat." This smoked lamb or mutton is usually served with green beans, potatoes coated in a white béchamel sauce, and side of pickled red cabbage.

HALLACAS

Similar to tamales, hallacas have been made in Venezuela for Christmas since colonial times, when slaves and servants filled their cornmeal cakes with the leftovers from colonists' dinner tables.

JANSSONS FRESTELSE

On the holidays, Swedes serve 'Jansson's Temptation,' a casserole dish made from potatoes, onions, heavy cream, breadcrumbs, and sprats- small, oily fish similar to sardines.

JELLY DOUGHNUTS

Fried dough is also a big part of Hanukkah festivities. In Israel, many enjoy *sufganiyot* (jelly doughnuts), while in Morocco, orange-scented doughnuts are the traditional dessert.

JULESILD

In Denmark this special holiday herring is pickled and spiced with cinnamon, cloves and sandalwood, and usually eaten with rugbrød (Danish rye bread) and homemade remoulade.

KING CAKE

Across South America, a *king cake* is served on January 6th, the Epiphany (January 6), with a small treat or trinket baked into one piece. Whoever finds the prize receives good luck.

KRANSEKAKE

Danes and Norwegians serve this 'wreath cake' over the holidays: an almond-flavored cake formed into a Christmas tree with as many as 18 layers.

KUTIA

In the Ukraine, *kutia* is the first dish served as part of Sviata Vecheria, a 12 dish vegetarian feast that commemorates the 12 apostles. It's made from wheat berries, poppy seeds, dried fruit, and honey.

LANTTULAATIKKO

In Finland, *lanttulaatikko*, a spiced swede bake is the center of the feasting. The swede is boiled and mashed, then combined with double cream, breadcrumbs, nutmeg and treacle before baking.

LATKES

In Israel, this potato cake is fried until its golden and crispy and served during the Jewish celebration of Hanukkah.

LUTEFISK

Dating back to Viking Scandinavia, *Lutefisk* is dried whitefish, usually cod, that has been rehydrated by soaking in lye, and is enjoyed at Christmas.

MALVA PUDDING

This sponge cake containing apricot jam is South Africa's favorite holiday dessert, often made with brandy or Amarula, a South African cream liqueur made from marula fruit.

MELOMAKARONA

A traditional dish served in Greece is *melomakarona*, a sweet, honey-soaked cookie topped with ground walnuts.

MINCE PIES

The English have enjoyed mince pies during the holidays since the 13th century, when Crusaders brought back exotic spices like nutmeg and cinnamon.

OYSTERS

On Christmas Eve, the French enjoy a midnight feast called Reveillon, which includes foie gras and oysters.

PAN DE JAMÓN

Venezuela's sweet-savory bread is traditionally served on Christmas Eve. The long loaf is filled with roasted ham, raisins, and green olives, and often accompanies dishes such as hallacas and dulce de lechoza (a sweet papaya dessert).

PASTELES

A classic Puerto Rican Christmas dish, these pastries consist of ground pork and adobo-blended spice sauce, with the outside wrapped in a special masa dough made of grated green bananas, yautía, and spices.

PECAN PIE

The French popularized this dessert when they settled in New Orleans in 1718, but the earliest recipes were called Texas pecan pie and were made of custards topped with pecans.

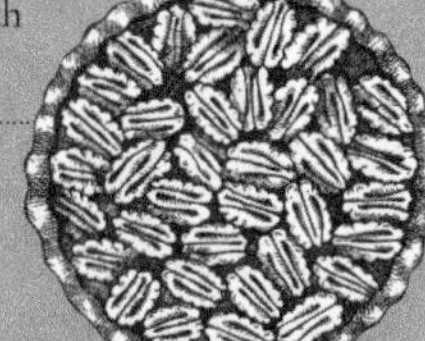

• HOLIDAY TREATS •
AROUND THE WORLD

PINNEKJØTT
Norway celebrates the holidays with wood-fired lamb ribs called *pinnekjøtt*. Traditional accompaniments include swede and carrot mash, and a sweet lingonberry jam. A shot of akevitt, a Scandanavian spirit spiced with fennel, caraway and star anise, completes the meal.

PONCHE NAVIDEÑO
– In Mexico, *ponche navideño*, or Christmas punch, is a festive drink made by simmering guava and apples with raw sugar cane, cinnamon and hibiscus. For a ponche con piquete ('punch with a sting'), add tequila.

PUMPKIN PIE
Pumpkins were first cultivated 9,000 years ago in Mexico and by Native Americans. The large gourds were roasted or boiled and often mixed with honey and spices and shaped into pie-like dishes.

PLUM PUDDING
Also known as Christmas pudding, this popular traditional holiday dish in the United Kingdom is typically made with dried fruit and spices, held together with eggs and suet. Some bake a coin inside and whoever finds it will have good luck in the new year.

PRIME RIB
This classic roast beef is a tradition Christmas dinner across the United States and is featured in the holiday movie 'The Grinch Who Stole Christmas.'

SAFFRON BUNS
Sweden and many Scandinavian countries celebrate St. Lucia's Day. One traditional ritual has the oldest daughter to dress in a white gown with a red sash and a crown of lit candles, and wake her parents with coffee and saffron buns.

SALTED CODFISH
In Portugal, Christmas Eve is celebrated with a meal called Consoada that includes dishes like salted codfish with potatoes. The food is left out overnight to feed the spirits of departed loved ones if they visit that night.

SHUBA
Known as 'herring under a fur coat,' *shuba* is a popular holiday dish in Russia. It includes pickled herring, hard-boiled eggs, mayonnaise, and grated vegetables like carrots, beets, potatoes, and onions.

SOPA DE GALETS
In Spain's Catalonia region, Christmas lunch features sopa de galets, a meaty soup bobbing with giant pasta shells from Catalonia.

SORPOTEL
In India's western state of Goa, an important Christmas Eve dish is *sorpotel*, a spicy stew consisting of pork liver and cinnamon, cumin and kashmiri chillies. Sana, coconut liqueur-infused rice cakes, often accompany the stew.

SPICED HOT CHOCOLATE
A Christmas tradition in Peru, where churches make large quantities of it and serve the hot beverage to the less fortunate.

STUFFING
The Romans first stuffed meats to add flavor, a practice later adopted by the Europeans, particularly the French. Today, stuffing is a popular side dish with turkey and gravy. When not cooked inside the turkey, it's called dressing.

TAMALES
Throughout Mexico and Costa Rica, *tamales* are the Christmas dish of choice.

TANGYUAN
During the Winter Solstice festival in China, these sweet or savory glutinous rice balls, filled with red bean paste, ground sesame or crushed peanuts, are traditionally made white, to mirror the moon.

TURKEY
A plump turkey is the traditional centerpiece of many American and British Christmas dinners, and enjoying the leftovers the day after is another holiday tradition.

WEIHNACHTSGANS
Since the Middle Ages, the traditional German Christmas feast centers around 'the Christmas goose,' which is often stuffed with apples, chestnuts, onions, and prunes.

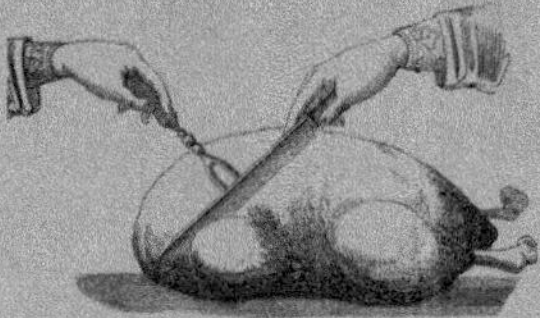

YEBEG WOT
A popular lamb stew served during the holiday season in Ethiopia, often served with onions, tomatoes, garlic, spices and kibbeh, an Ethiopian butter.

Holiday Memories

Place your holiday card or picture here

Where we spent the holidays

What the weather was like

What was happening in the world

What filled us with holiday spirit this year

Place a picture of
your Christmas tree here

A favorite tradition celebrated

Thanksgiving

Christmas Eve

• KRAMPUS •

(AUSTRIA)

In Austria, *Krampus* is the evil accomplice of Saint Nicholas. As the pagan legend goes, on December 6 this ghoulish half-man, half-goat demon begins to roam the streets frightening children and punishing the bad ones. Today, Austrians dress up as Krampus throughout the month of December scaring little ones and pulling ghastly pranks. The annual Krampus Parade in Vienna is one of Europe's most popular festivals.

Decorating memories

Christmas Day

Favorite foods and meals

Favorite gifts

Favorite songs this year

Favorite movies and books this year

Memorable trips, parties, and events

COLUMBIA

To honor the Virgin Mary, candles and paper lanterns are placed in windows, balconies and front yards. Called *Día de las Velitas*, or Little Candles' Day, entire towns and cities are lit up in festive displays.

Place the favorite greeting card you received here

One moment we will always treasure

Special acts of kindess

Special visitors we welcomed

The New Year

• HOLIDAY MOVIES •

Watching holiday movies is a tradition for many around the world, especially in the United States. Which of these 140 films are your holiday favorites?

Movie Title	*Always Watch*	*Sometimes Watch*	*Might Watch*	*Won't Watch*
12 Dates of Christmas (2011 TV Movie, PG) A story that follows Kate, a young woman who after a horrible blind date on Christmas Eve, wakes up to find she is re-living that same day and date all over again.	○	○	○	○
12 Days of Giving (2017 TV Movie, G) After winning a $50,000 prize, a man decides to pay things forward by buying Christmas gifts for strangers under the pseudonym, Lucky the Elf.	○	○	○	○
8-Bit Christmas (2021, PG) In 1980s Chicago, a 10-year-old sets out on a quest to get the Christmas gift of his generation: the latest and greatest video-game system.	○	○	○	○
A Bad Moms Christmas (2017, R) As their own mothers drop in unexpectedly, our three under-appreciated and over-burdened moms rebel against the challenges and expectations of the Super Bowl for mothers: Christmas.	○	○	○	○
A Boy Called Christmas (2021, PG) In this origin story of Father Christmas, an ordinary boy (with a loyal pet mouse and a reindeer at his side) sets out on an extraordinary adventure to find his father who is on a quest to discover the fabled village of Elfhelm.	○	○	○	○
A Boyfriend for Christmas (2004 TV Movie, G) On Christmas Day, Santa brings two lonely people together. But can love overcome deception?	○	○	○	○
A Charlie Brown Christmas (1965 TV Movie, G) Depressed at the commercialism he sees around him, Charlie Brown tries to find a deeper meaning to Christmas.	○	○	○	○
A Christmas Carol (1951, PG) Ebenezer Scrooge, a curmudgeonly, miserly businessman, has no time for sentimentality and largely views Christmas as a waste of time. However, this Christmas Eve he will be visited by three spirits who will show him the errors of his ways. The movie has been remade several times.	○	○	○	○

Movie Title	*Always Watch*	*Sometimes Watch*	*Might Watch*	*Won't Watch*
A Christmas Prince (2017, PG) When a reporter goes undercover as a tutor to get the inside scoop on a playboy prince, she gets tangled in some royal intrigue and ends up finding love - but will she be able to keep up her lie?	○	○	○	○
A Christmas Story (1983, PG) In the 1940s, a young boy named Ralphie Parker attempts to convince his parents, teacher, and Santa Claus that a Red Ryder Range 200 Shot BB gun really is the perfect Christmas gift.	○	○	○	○
A Christmas Story Christmas (2022, PG) Follows the now-adult Ralphie as he returns to the house on Cleveland Street to give his kids a magical Christmas like the one he had as a child, reconnecting with childhood friends, and reconciling the passing of his Old Man.	○	○	○	○
A Christmas Tale (2008, Not Rated) The troubled Vuillard family is no stranger to illness, grief, and banishment, but when their matriarch requires a bone-marrow transplant, the estranged clan reunites just in time for Christmas.	○	○	○	○
A Grandpa for Christmas (2007 TV Movie, PG) Bert O'Reiley is a retired song and dance man who becomes an instant grandfather to the nine-year-old granddaughter he has never met.	○	○	○	○
A Season for Miracles (1999 TV Movie, G) A miracle occurs for a homeless family consisting of two children neglected by their incarcerated mother and their protective aunt who is trying to keep them out of the foster system with the help of an angel.	○	○	○	○
A Very Harold & Kumar Christmas (2011, R) Six years after their Guantanamo Bay adventure, stoner buds Harold Lee and Kumar Patel cause a holiday fracas by inadvertently burning down Harold's father-in-law's prize Christmas tree.	○	○	○	○
All I Want Is Christmas (2012, PG) A Christmas obsessed Jewish boy on his way to sunny Florida figures out how to get the Christmas of his dreams by trading airline tickets and places with another boy on his way to snowy Christmastown, WA.	○	○	○	○

Movie Title	*Always Watch*	*Sometimes Watch*	*Might Watch*	*Won't Watch*
All I Want for Christmas (1991, G) A brother and sister attempt to bring their divorced parents back together for Christmas.	○	○	○	○
Almost Christmas (2016, PG-13) A dysfunctional family gathers together for their first Christmas since their mom died.	○	○	○	○
Arthur Christmas (2011, PG) Santa's clumsy son Arthur sets out on a mission with Grandsanta to give out a present they misplaced to a young girl in less than two hours.	○	○	○	○
Babes in Toyland (1961, Not Rated) Mary Contrary is set to marry Tom Piper when he is kidnapped by Roderigo and Gonzorgo, two goons working for the evil Barnaby who wants to marry Mary for her inheritance.	○	○	○	○
Bad Santa (2003, R) A miserable conman and his partner pose as Santa and his Little Helper to rob department stores on Christmas Eve. But they run into problems when the conman befriends a troubled kid.	○	○	○	○
Bad Santa 2 (2016, R) Fueled by cheap whiskey, greed and hatred, Willie teams up once again with his angry little sidekick, Marcus, to knock off a Chicago charity on Christmas Eve.	○	○	○	○
Batman Returns (1992, PG-13) While Batman deals with a deformed man calling himself the Penguin wreaking havoc across Gotham with the help of a cruel businessman, a female employee of the latter becomes the Catwoman with her own vendetta.	○	○	○	○
Beyond Tomorrow (1940, Not Rated) The ghosts of three elderly industrialists killed in an airplane crash return to Earth to help reunite a young couple they initially brought together.	○	○	○	○
Christmas Mail (2010, PG) In this holiday romantic comedy, a mysterious woman who works at the post office answering Santa's mail captures the heart of a disillusioned postal carrier	○	○	○	○
Christmas in Boston (2005 TV Movie, G) Gina and Seth have been pen pals for 13 years and now will have the chance to meet. Both used their best friends pictures to send to each other and now will let their friends meet.	○	○	○	○
Christmas in Connecticut (1945, Not Rated) A food writer who has lied about being the perfect housewife must try to cover her deception when her boss and a returning war hero invite themselves to her home for a traditional family Christmas.	○	○	○	○
Christmas with the Kranks (2004, PG) With their daughter, Blair, away in Peru, Luther and Nora Krank decide to skip Christmas all together until she decides to come home, causing an uproar when they have to celebrate it at the last minute.	○	○	○	○

Movie Title	*Always Watch*	*Sometimes Watch*	*Might Watch*	*Won't Watch*
Crown for Christmas (2015 TV Movie, G) After getting fired from her job as a maid at a ritzy New York City hotel, Allie reluctantly accepts a temporary gig as the governess to a young girl who is part of a powerful family in Europe that lives in a castle.	○	○	○	○
Deck the Halls (2006, PG) Two neighbors have it out after one of them decorates his house for the holidays so brightly that it can be seen from space.	○	○	○	○
Die Hard (1988, R) A New York City police officer tries to save his estranged wife and several others taken hostage by terrorists during a Christmas party at the Nakatomi Plaza in Los Angeles. Die Hard 2 (1990, R) also takes place over Christmas.	○	○	○	○
Disney's A Christmas Carol (2009, PG) An animated retelling of Charles Dickens' classic novel about a Victorian-era miser taken on a journey of self-redemption, courtesy of several mysterious Christmas apparitions.	○	○	○	○
Dolly Parton's Christmas on the Square (2020, PG-13) An embittered scrooge of a woman plans to sell her small town, regardless of the consequences to the people who live there. However, a kindhearted angel arrives and shows her what would happen before she mends her ways and redeems herself.	○	○	○	○
Edward Scissorhands (1990, PG-13) An artificial man, who was incompletely constructed and has scissors for hands, leads a solitary life. Then one day, a suburban lady meets him and introduces him to her world.	○	○	○	○
Elf (2003, PG) Raised as an oversized elf, Buddy travels from the North Pole to New York City to meet his biological father, Walter Hobbs, who doesn't know he exists and is in desperate need of some Christmas spirit.	○	○	○	○
Eloise at Christmastime (2003, G) A 6-year-old girl tries to reunite a young woman with a former boyfriend before she marries another.	○	○	○	○
Ernest Saves Christmas (1988, PG) Ernest helps Santa Claus as he searches for his successor.	○	○	○	○
Falling for Christmas (2022, PG) In the days leading up to Christmas, a young and newly engaged heiress experiences a skiing accident. After being diagnosed with amnesia, she finds herself in the care of the handsome lodge owner and his daughter.	○	○	○	○
Fatman (2020, R) A rowdy, unorthodox Santa Claus is fighting to save his declining business. Meanwhile, Billy, a neglected and precocious 12-year-old, hires a hit man to kill Santa after receiving a lump of coal in his stocking.	○	○	○	○
Four Christmases (2008, PG-13) A couple struggles to visit all four of their divorced parents on Christmas.	○	○	○	○

Movie Title	Always Watch	Sometimes Watch	Might Watch	Won't Watch
Fred Claus (2007, PG) Fred Claus, Santa's bitter older brother, is forced to move to the North Pole to help Santa and the elves prepare for Christmas in exchange for cash.	○	○	○	○
Friday After Next (2002, R) Working as security guards, Craig and Day-Day run into the thief who stole their Christmas presents.	○	○	○	○
Frosty the Snowman (1969 TV Movie, G) A living snowman and a little girl struggle to elude a greedy magician who is after the snowman's magic hat.	○	○	○	○
Gremlins (1984, PG) A young man inadvertently breaks three important rules concerning his new pet and unleashes a horde of malevolently mischievous monsters on a small town.	○	○	○	○
Grumpy Cat's Worst Christmas Ever (2014 TV Movie, G) Grumpy Cat is an Internet meme sensation with over 6 million Facebook friends, who has graced the cover of New York Magazine, is the spokescat for Friskies, appeared on American Idol and the MTV Movie Awards.	○	○	○	○
Happiest Season (2020, PG-13) A holiday romantic comedy that captures the range of emotions tied to wanting your family's acceptance, being true to yourself, and trying not to ruin Christmas by revealing a nasty secret.	○	○	○	○
Harry Potter and the Sorcerer's Stone (2001, PG) An orphaned boy enrolls in a school of wizardry, where he learns the truth about himself, his family and the terrible evil that haunts the magical world.	○	○	○	○
Holidate (2020, PG) Fed up with being single on holidays, two strangers agree to be each other's platonic plus-ones all year long, only to catch real feelings along the way.	○	○	○	○
Holiday Affair (1949, Not Rated) A young widow is torn between a boring attorney and a romantic ne'er-do-well.	○	○	○	○
Holiday in Handcuffs (2006 TV Movie, Not Rated) A struggling artist working as a waitress kidnaps one of her customers to take home to meet her parents at Christmastime.	○	○	○	○
Holiday Inn (1942, Not Rated) At an inn which is open only on holidays, a crooner and a hoofer vie for the affections of a beautiful up-and-coming performer.	○	○	○	○
Home Alone (1990, PG) An eight-year-old troublemaker must protect his house from a pair of burglars when he is accidentally left home alone by his family during Christmas vacation.	○	○	○	○

Movie Title	Always Watch	Sometimes Watch	Might Watch	Won't Watch
Home Alone 2: Lost in New York (1992, PG) One year after Kevin McCallister was left home alone and had to defeat a pair of bumbling burglars, he accidentally finds himself stranded in New York City - and the same criminals are not far behind.	○	○	○	○
How the Grinch Stole Christmas! (1966 TV Movie, Not Rated) A grumpy hermit hatches a plan to steal Christmas from the Whos of Whoville.	○	○	○	○
How the Grinch Stole Christmas (2000, PG) On the outskirts of Whoville lives a green, revenge-seeking Grinch who plans to ruin Christmas for all of the citizens of the town.	○	○	○	○
I'll Be Home for Christmas (1998, PG) A college student faces an impossible journey when he is left stranded in the desert, thousands of miles from home, with no money and only a few days left until Christmas.	○	○	○	○
It Happened on Fifth Avenue (1947, Not Rated) Two homeless men move into a mansion while its owners are wintering in the South.	○	○	○	○
It's a Wonderful Life (1946, PG) An angel is sent from Heaven to help a desperately frustrated businessman by showing him what life would have been like if he had never existed.	○	○	○	○
Jack Frost (1998, PG) A father who can't keep his promises is killed in a car accident. One year later, he returns as a snowman who has the final chance to put things right with his son before he is gone forever.	○	○	○	○
Jingle All the Way (1996, PG) A father vows to get his son a Turbo Man action figure for Christmas. However, every store is sold out, and he must travel all over town and compete with everybody else in order to find one.	○	○	○	○
Jingle Jangle: A Christmas Journey (2020, PG) An imaginary world comes to life in a holiday tale of an eccentric toymaker, his adventurous granddaughter, and a magical invention that has the power to change their lives forever.	○	○	○	○
Joyeux Noel (2005, PG-13) In December 1914, an unofficial Christmas truce on the Western Front allows soldiers from opposing sides of the First World War to gain insight into each other's way of life.	○	○	○	○
Just Friends (2005, PG-13) While visiting his hometown during Christmas, a man comes face-to-face with his old high school crush whom he was best friends with -- a woman whose rejection of him turned him into a ferocious womanizer.	○	○	○	○
Klaus (2019, PG) A simple act of kindness always sparks another, even in a frozen, faraway place. When Smeerensburg's new postman, Jesper, befriends toymaker Klaus, their gifts melt an age-old feud and deliver a sleigh full of holiday traditions.	○	○	○	○

Movie Title	*Always Watch*	*Sometimes Watch*	*Might Watch*	*Won't Watch*

Krampus
(2015, PG-13) A horror film in which a boy who has a bad Christmas accidentally summons a festive demon to his family home.

Kristin's Christmas Past
(2013 TV Movie, PG) Given the opportunity to visit her estranged family on Christmas Eve 1996, Kristin Cartwright hopes to change her past in order to improve her current life in 2013.

Last Christmas
(2019, PG-13) Kate is a young woman subscribed to bad decisions. Working as an elf in a year round Christmas store is not good for the wannabe singer. However, she meets Tom there. Her life takes a new turn. For Kate, it seems too good to be true.

Last Holiday
(2006, PG-13) Upon learning of a terminal illness, a shy woman decides to sell all her possessions and live it up at a posh Central European hotel.

Little Women
(1949, Not Rated) The four daughters of a New England family fight for happiness during and after the Civil War.

Love Actually
(2003, R) Follows the lives of eight very different couples in dealing with their love lives in various loosely interrelated tales all set during a frantic month before Christmas in London, England.

Lovely, Still
(2008, PG) A holiday fable that tells the story of an elderly man discovering love for the first time.

Meet Me in St. Louis
(1944, Not Rated) Young love and childish fears highlight a year in the life of a turn-of-the-century family.

Mickey's Christmas Carol
(1983, G) The classic Disney animated characters play the roles in this animated retelling of the Charles Dickens masterpiece.

Miracle on 34th Street
(1947, Not Rated) After a divorced New York mother hires a nice old man to play Santa Claus at Macy's, she is startled by his claim to be the genuine article. When his sanity is questioned, a lawyer defends him in court by arguing that he's not mistaken. The movie has been remade several times.

Mixed Nuts
(1994, PG-13) The events focus around a crisis hotline business on one crazy night during the Christmas holidays.

Mrs. Miracle
(2009 TV Movie, Not Rated) Overwhelmed widower Seth Webster is searching for a housekeeper to help him with his unruly six year old twin sons. "Mrs. Miracle" mysteriously appears and quickly becomes an irreplaceable nanny, chef, friend... and matchmaker.

Movie Title	*Always Watch*	*Sometimes Watch*	*Might Watch*	*Won't Watch*

National Lampoon's Christmas Vacation
(1989, PG-13) The Griswold family's plans for a big family Christmas predictably turn into a big disaster.

Nativity!
(2009, PG) An uptight but secretly heartbroken primary school teacher's little white lie about Hollywood coming to see his class' Nativity play grows like wildfire in his rag-tag school low on self-esteem.

Next Stop, Christmas
(2021 TV Movie, G) Angie is determined to spend Christmas alone but her usual commuter ride turns into a Christmas train that drops her off in her home town in 2011.

Noel
(2004, PG) Five New Yorkers come together on Christmas Eve, seeking a miracle.

Noelle
(2019, G) Santa's daughter must take over the family business when her father retires and her brother, who is supposed to inherit the Santa role, gets cold feet.

Nothing Like the Holidays
(2008, PG-13) A Puerto Rican family living in the area of Humboldt Park in west Chicago face what may be their last Christmas together.

November Christmas
(2010 TV Movie, G) A brave young girl's battle against cancer has an effect on the people around her.

Office Christmas Party
(2016, R) When his uptight CEO sister threatens to shut down his branch, the branch manager throws an epic Christmas party in order to land a big client and save the day, but the party gets way out of hand...

One Magic Christmas
(1985, G) An angel must show a mother the true meaning of Christmas. It's not just presents and materialistic things, but the people she cares about.

Operation Christmas Drop
(2020, G) Congressional aide Erica forgoes family Christmas to travel at her boss's behest. At a beach side Air Force base, she clashes with Capt. Andrew Jantz, who knows her assignment is finding reasons to defund the facility.

Pete's Christmas
(2013 TV Movie, PG) A put-upon teen finds himself reliving the same miserable Christmas day over and over again.

Planes, Trains & Automobiles
(1987, R) A Chicago advertising man must struggle to travel home from New York for Thanksgiving, with a lovable oaf of a shower-curtain-ring salesman as his only companion

Prancer
(1989, G) A farm girl nurses a wounded reindeer she believes is one of Santa's, hoping to bring it back to health in time for Christmas. Her holiday spirit inspires those around her, something her disheartened father is having trouble understanding.

Movie Title	Always Watch	Sometimes Watch	Might Watch	Won't Watch
Remember the Night (1940, Not Rated) Love blooms between a sympathetic attorney and the comely shoplifter he has taken home for the Christmas holiday.	○	○	○	○
Rudolph the Red-Nosed Reindeer (1964 TV Movie, G) Young reindeer Rudolph lives at the North Pole. His father is one of Santa's reindeer and it is expected that Rudolph will eventually be one too. However, he has a feature which is a setback and causes him to be ostracized: his red nose.	○	○	○	○
Santa Claus Is Comin' to Town (1970 TV Movie, G) A mailman reveals the origin of Santa Claus.	○	○	○	○
Santa Claus: The Movie (1985, PG) The legend of Santa Claus is put in jeopardy when an unscrupulous toy manufacturer attempts to take over Christmas.	○	○	○	○
Scrooged (1988, PG-13) A selfish, cynical television executive is haunted by three spirits bearing lessons on Christmas Eve.	○	○	○	○
Serendipity (2001, PG-13) A couple search for each other years after the night they first met, fell in love, and separated, convinced that one day they'd end up together.	○	○	○	○
Shazam! (2019, PG-13) A newly fostered young boy in search of his mother instead finds unexpected super powers and soon gains a powerful enemy.	○	○	○	○
Silent Night (2002 TV Movie, PG) In a cabin in a WWII front, a German mom with a son mediates a truce between 3 German and 3 American soldiers so they can all celebrate Christmas Eve 1944 together.	○	○	○	○
Surviving Christmas (2004, PG-13) A lonely, obnoxious young millionaire pays a family to spend Christmas with him.	○	○	○	○
The Apartment (1960, Not Rated) A Manhattan insurance clerk tries to rise in his company by letting its executives use his apartment for trysts, but complications and a romance of his own ensue.	○	○	○	○
The Best Man Holiday (2013, R) When college friends reunite after 15 years over the Christmas holidays, they discover just how easy it is for long-forgotten rivalries and romances to be reignited.	○	○	○	○
The Bishop's Wife (1947, Not Rated) A debonair angel comes to Earth to help an Episcopalian bishop and his wife in their quest to raise money for the new church.	○	○	○	○
The Christmas Card (2006 TV Movie, G) A US soldier visits the town from where an inspirational Christmas card was sent to him by a church group that mails cards out to servicemen as a goodwill effort.	○	○	○	○

Movie Title	Always Watch	Sometimes Watch	Might Watch	Won't Watch
The Christmas Chronicles (2018, PG) The story of sister and brother, Kate and Teddy Pierce, whose Christmas Eve plan to catch Santa Claus on camera turns into an unexpected journey that most kids could only dream about.	○	○	○	○
The Christmas Chronicles: Part Two (2020, PG) Kate Pierce, now a cynical teen, is unexpectedly reunited with Santa Claus when a mysterious troublemaker threatens to cancel Christmas - forever.	○	○	○	○
The Christmas Shoes (2002 TV Movie, PG) A young boy tries to get a pair of Christmas shoes for his dying mother, while a lawyer tries to deal with the break-up of his marriage.	○	○	○	○
The Chronicles of Narnia: The Lion, the Witch and the Wardrobe (2005, PG) Four kids travel through a wardrobe to the land of Narnia and learn of their destiny to free it with the guidance of a mystical lion.	○	○	○	○
The Disappearance of Haruhi Suzumiya (2010, Not Rated) A week before Christmas, Kyon wakes up in a world where the SOS Brigade doesn't exist. Mikuru and Yuki don't recognize him, and Haruhi and Itsuki seem to have vanished.	○	○	○	○
The Family Man (2000, PG-13) A fast-lane investment broker, offered the opportunity to see how the other half lives, wakes up to find that his sports car and girlfriend have become a mini-van and wife.	○	○	○	○
The Family Stone (2005, PG-13) An uptight, conservative businesswoman accompanies her boyfriend to his eccentric and outgoing family's annual Christmas celebration and finds that she's a fish out of water in their free-spirited way of life.	○	○	○	○
The Great Rupert (1950, Not Rated) A little squirrel with lots of charm accidentally helps two poor, down-but-NOT-out families overcome their obstacles.	○	○	○	○
The Grinch (2018, PG) A grumpy Grinch plots to ruin Christmas for the village of Whoville.	○	○	○	○
The Holiday (2006, PG-13) Two women troubled with guy-problems swap homes in each other's countries, where they each meet a local guy and fall in love.				
The House Without a Christmas Tree (1972 TV Movie, Not Rated) In 1946 Nebraska, a young girl named Addie desperately craves a Christmas tree, but her bitter widower father refuses because of events from the family's past.	○	○	○	○
The Lemon Drop Kid (1951, Not Rated) A New York City swindler has until Christmas to come up with the $10,000 he owes a gangster, prompting him to go into scamming overdrive.	○	○	○	○

Movie Title	Always Watch	Sometimes Watch	Might Watch	Won't Watch
The Little Drummer Boy (1968 TV Movie, Not Rated) An orphan drummer boy who hates humanity finds his life changed forever when he meets three wise men en route to Bethlehem.	○	○	○	○
The Man Who Invented Christmas (2017, PG) The journey that led to Charles Dickens' creation of 'A Christmas Carol', a timeless tale that would redefine Christmas.	○	○	○	○
The Most Wonderful Time of the Year (2008 TV Movie, PG) Corporate analyst and single mom, Jen, tackles Christmas with a business-like approach until her uncle arrives with a handsome stranger in tow.	○	○	○	○
The Muppet Christmas Carol (1992, G) The Muppets present their own touching rendition of Charles Dickens' classic tale.	○	○	○	○
The Nativity Story (2005, PG) A drama that focuses on the period in Mary and Joseph's life where they journeyed to Bethlehem for the birth of Jesus.	○	○	○	○
The Night Before (2015, R) On Christmas Eve, three lifelong friends spend the night in New York City looking for the Holy Grail of Christmas parties.	○	○	○	○
The Nightmare Before Christmas (1993, PG) Jack Skellington, king of Halloween Town, discovers Christmas Town, but his attempts to bring Christmas to his home causes confusion.	○	○	○	○
The Polar Express (2004, G) On Christmas Eve, a young boy embarks on a magical adventure to the North Pole on the Polar Express, while learning about friendship, bravery, and the spirit of Christmas.	○	○	○	○
The Princess Switch (2018, PG) Competing in a Christmas baking competition in Belgravia, a Chicago baker bumps into the prince's fiancée--who looks just like her. They switch lives for two days.	○	○	○	○
The Ref (1994, R) A cat burglar is forced to take a bickering, dysfunctional family hostage on Christmas Eve.	○	○	○	○
The Santa Clause (1994, PG) When a man inadvertently makes Santa fall off his roof on Christmas Eve, he finds himself magically recruited to take his place.	○	○	○	○
The Santa Clause 2 (2002, G) Scott Calvin has been a humble Santa Claus for eight years, but it might come to an end if he doesn't find a Mrs. Claus.	○	○	○	○
The Santa Clause 3: Escape Clause (2006, G) Santa, a.k.a. Scott Calvin, is faced with double-duty: how to keep his new family happy and how to stop Jack Frost from taking over Christmas.	○	○	○	○
The Shop Around the Corner (1940, Not Rated) Two employees at a gift shop can barely stand each other, without realizing that they are falling in love through the post as each other's anonymous pen pal.	○	○	○	○

Movie Title	Always Watch	Sometimes Watch	Might Watch	Won't Watch
The Snowman (1982 TV Movie, G) On Christmas Eve, a young boy builds a snowman that comes to life and takes him to the North Pole to meet Father Christmas.	○	○	○	○
The Ultimate Christmas Present (2000 TV Movie, G) A girl steals a weather machine from Santa Claus, to make a snow day. The machine breaks, and causes an out-of-control snowstorm.	○	○	○	○
The Year Without a Santa Claus (1974 TV Movie, G) When a weary and discouraged Santa Claus considers skipping his Christmas Eve run one year, Mrs. Claus and his elves set out to change his mind.	○	○	○	○
This Christmas (2007, PG-13) A Christmastime drama centered around the Whitfield family's first holiday together in four years.	○	○	○	○
Tokyo Godfathers (2003, PG-13) On Christmas Eve, three homeless people living on the streets of Tokyo discover a newborn baby among the trash and set out to find its parents.	○	○	○	○
Trading Places (1983, R) A snobbish investor and a wily street con artist find their positions reversed as part of a bet by two callous millionaires.	○	○	○	○
Trapped in Paradise (1994, PG-13) Residents of a friendly Pennsylvania town foil three brothers' plan to r ob a bank on Christmas Eve.	○	○	○	○
Violent Night (2022, R) When a group of mercenaries attack the estate of a wealthy family, Santa Claus must step in to save the day (and Christmas).	○	○	○	○
White Christmas (1954, Not Rated) A successful song-and-dance team become romantically involved with a sister act and team up to save the failing Vermont inn of their former commanding general.	○	○	○	○
Window Wonderland (2013 TV Movie, G) A department-store window decorator learns there is a vacancy for her dream job in the run-up to Christmas, only to find a professional rival has his eye on it too.	○	○	○	○

Holiday Memories

(YEAR)

Place your holiday card or picture here

Where we spent the holidays

What the weather was like

What was happening in the world

What filled us with holiday spirit this year

Place a picture of
your Christmas tree here

A favorite tradition celebrated

Thanksgiving

Decorating memories

• KENTUCKY FRIED CHICKEN •

(JAPAN)

Christmas is not an official holiday in Japan, but many Japanese now celebrate the holiday by eating buckets of Kentucky Fried Chicken. In the 1970s, the manager of the first KFC in Japan began marketing fried chicken as a holiday dinner for foreigners who missed having turkey for Christmas. In 1974, the American fast-food chain launched a campaign called "Kurisumasu ni wa kentakkii!" or "Kentucky for Christmas!" An estimated four million families across Japan now celebrate Christmas with a bucket of chicken from the white-bearded Colonel Sanders.

Christmas Eve

Christmas Day

Favorite foods and meals

Favorite gifts

Favorite songs this year

Favorite movies and books this year

Memorable trips, parties, and events

SWITZERLAND

Swiss families create their own Advent calendars together, with each day revealing a new surprise or treat.

Place the favorite greeting card you received here

One moment we will always treasure

Special acts of kindess

Special visitors we welcomed

The New Year

• HOLIDAY TRADITIONS •

The holidays are a joyous time steeped in traditions, both new and old. How many of these common Christmas traditions to do celebrate?

Tradition	Every Year	Some Years	Might Do	Won't Do
Visit Santa Claus	○	○	○	○
Have a large dinner feast	○	○	○	○
Hang mistletoe	○	○	○	○
Light a yule log	○	○	○	○
Hang stockings	○	○	○	○
Hang electric lights outside	○	○	○	○
Decorate with garland or evergreen branches	○	○	○	○
Sing carols	○	○	○	○
Give gifts	○	○	○	○
Decorate with Poinsettias	○	○	○	○
Bake holiday cookies	○	○	○	○
Send out greeting cards	○	○	○	○
Light a yule candle	○	○	○	○
Drink from a Wassail bowl	○	○	○	○
Go to a holiday party	○	○	○	○
Buy a Christmas tree	○	○	○	○

Tradition	Every Year	Some Years	Might Do	Won't Do
Decorate a Christas tree	○	○	○	○
Gift Christmas pajamas on Christmas Eve	○	○	○	○
Read 'Twas the Night before Christmas'	○	○	○	○
String popcorn for the Christmas tree	○	○	○	○
Drive around to see Christmas lights	○	○	○	○
Make colorful paper chains for the Christmas tree	○	○	○	○
Watch A Christmas Carol	○	○	○	○
Hang a pickle ornament	○	○	○	○
Drink hot chocolate	○	○	○	○
Leave magic reindeer food out	○	○	○	○
Watch holiday movies	○	○	○	○
Take a picture in front of your Christmas tree	○	○	○	○

Tradition	*Every Year*	*Some Years*	*Might Do*	*Won't Do*
Attend a Christmas parade	○	○	○	○
Write in the Holiday Memories book	○	○	○	○
Track Santa on Christmas Eve	○	○	○	○
Volunteer	○	○	○	○
Buy a special ornament	○	○	○	○
Attend a Christmas concert	○	○	○	○
Use Christmas dinnerware and serving trays	○	○	○	○
Make a gingerbread house	○	○	○	○
Have a snowball fight	○	○	○	○
Leave milk and cookies for Santa	○	○	○	○
See a holiday play	○	○	○	○
Go ice skating	○	○	○	○
Visit a Nativity display	○	○	○	○
Go to Christmas mass	○	○	○	○
Deliver cookies to local service providers	○	○	○	○
Elf on the Shelf	○	○	○	○
Christmas puzzle night	○	○	○	○
Build a snowman	○	○	○	○
Go Sledding	○	○	○	○
Make pomanders	○	○	○	○
Make paper snowflakes	○	○	○	○
Make snow angels	○	○	○	○
Wear an ugly holiday sweater	○	○	○	○

Tradition	*Every Year*	*Some Years*	*Might Do*	*Won't Do*
Wrap gifts	○	○	○	○
Visit a tree farm	○	○	○	○
Take holiday family photos	○	○	○	○
Go see The Nutcracker	○	○	○	○
Write a letter to Santa	○	○	○	○
Go to a tree lighting ceremony	○	○	○	○
Sing The Twelve Days of Christmas	○	○	○	○
Countdown with an Advent Calendar	○	○	○	○
Make gingerbread men	○	○	○	○
Display Christmas cards	○	○	○	○
Watch Macy's Thanksgiving Day parade	○	○	○	○
Make gifts	○	○	○	○
Adopt a charity	○	○	○	○
Host a Christmas party	○	○	○	○
Open one gift on Christmas Eve	○	○	○	○
Have a family game night	○	○	○	○
Have a Christmas cookie decorating contest	○	○	○	○
Sing Christmas karaoke	○	○	○	○
Dress up your pet	○	○	○	○
Make your own Christmas cards	○	○	○	○
Personalize Christmas stockings	○	○	○	○
Bake with peppermint	○	○	○	○

Holiday Memories

....

(YEAR)

Place your holiday card or picture here

Where we spent the holidays

What the weather was like

What was happening in the world

What filled us with holiday spirit this year

Place a picture of
your Christmas tree here

A favorite tradition celebrated

Thanksgiving

Decorating memories

Christmas Eve

Christmas Day

Favorite gifts

Favorite foods and meals

Favorite songs this year

COSTA RICA

While in most of the world the poinsettia is the most common flower of Christmas, in Costa Roca the official Christmas flower is the orchid.

• CHRISTMAS • CATERPILLARS

(SOUTH AFRICA)

For the holidays, families in South Africa come together for braaing, a Christmas cookout of steaks, boerewors sausages, and a South African specialty: sundried Emperor Moth caterpillars. The creepy crawly delicacy is fried or sundried and covered in festive colors. A terrific source of protein and surprisingly nutritious, the 'Christmas Caterpillar' it is said to bring good fortune in the new year for anyone who can swallow one.

Memorable trips, parties, and events

Favorite movies and books this year

Place the favorite greeting card you received here

One moment we will always treasure

Special acts of kindness

Special visitors we welcomed

The New Year

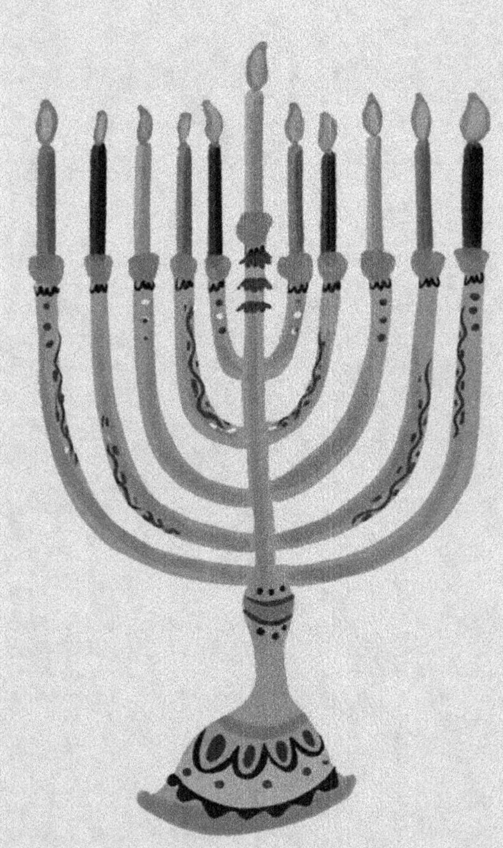

Holiday Memories

Place your holiday card or picture here

Where we spent the holidays

What the weather was like

What was happening in the world

What filled us with holiday spirit this year

Place a picture of
your Christmas tree here

A favorite tradition celebrated

Thanksgiving

Decorating memories

Christmas Eve

Christmas Day

DENMARK

On St. Lucia Day, December 13th, the oldest daughter in the family dresses in a white gown and wears a crown made from twigs with nine candles.

Favorite foods and meals

Favorite gifts

Favorite songs this year

Memorable trips, parties, and events

Favorite movies and books this year

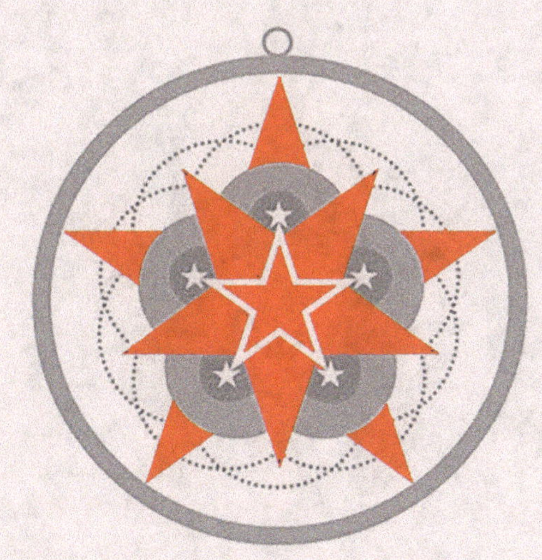

• LANTERNS •

(PHILIPPINES)

For the longest Christmas celebration in the world, head to the Philippines, where holiday light displays and festivals run from September through January. Every year the city of San Fernando, the 'Christmas capital of the Philippines,' holds the Giant Lantern Festival (*Ligligan Parul Sampernandu*). 'Parols,' Christmas lanterns symbolizing the Star of Bethlehem, are made from bamboo and paper and festoon towns and villages. Some are over twenty-feet tall and are illuminated by thousands of spinning lights that sparkle in kaleidoscope patterns.

Place the favorite greeting card you received here

One moment we will always treasure

Special acts of kindess

Special visitors we welcomed

The New Year

Holiday Memories

Place your holiday card or picture here

Where we spent the holidays

What the weather was like

What was happening in the world

What filled us with holiday spirit this year

Place a picture of
your Christmas tree here

A favorite tradition celebrated

Thanksgiving

Christmas Eve

• ROLLER SKATING •

(VENEZUELA)

On Christmas morning in Caracas, Venezuela, roads are closed and city-dwellers go to church on roller skates 'en masse.' The skating congregation has become a popular annual ritual. It is said that children go to bed with a skate lace tied to their toe and the other end dangling out the window, so that when friends skate by, they can tug at the lace so the sleepy child knows it's time to get their skates on and go to mass.

Favorite foods and meals

Favorite gifts

• CRACKERS •
(UNITED KINGDOM)

Across Britain, crackers are a mainstay of the Christmas holidays. The carboard tube with three chambers is covered and twisted in holiday paper – the middle chamber filled with prizes: a small toy, riddles, candy, and most importantly, a paper crown. The crown is a nod to the ancient Romans who wore festive headgear to celebrate Saturnalia, the winter solstice and precursor to Christmas. When two people tug at each end of the cracker, it breaks in two with a loud 'crack!' Whoever is holding the largest end receives the prizes inside.

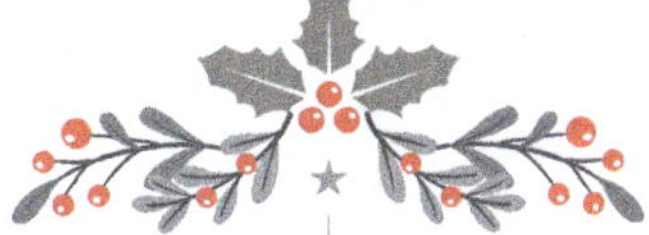

Favorite songs this year

Memorable trips, parties, and events

IRELAND

In the front window of Irish homes, a tall red candle is kept lit to welcome warmth and shelter for the holiday season.

Favorite movies and books this year

One moment we will always treasure

Special acts of kindess

Special visitors we welcomed

The New Year

Edwin Kim

Illustrated By
Mayara Nogueira

Tae watches a popular band perform and witnesses the exciting energy of the crowd. It's now his turn on stage, and the audience becomes dead silent. To his surprise, they make fun of Tae, and he runs away in sadness. He always felt different, but never expected to feel so rejected.

While alone, he hears a voice. He follows the voice and finds Ruby, the robin. Ruby tells Tae about Tiger Town - a place where everyone looks just like him. Immediately, he decides he must travel there. Will he make it to Tiger Town? Will he feel truly accepted? Read to find out more!

Tae the Tiger was feeling very strange.
He felt tingly and twitchy.
Shivery and sweaty.
His head was swimming, and his
tummy was full of butterflies.
Tae wasn't sick, and he wasn't sad.
He was feeling nervous and really
excited at the same time.

Today was the day!
It’s, “HORSE CITY’S GREATEST TALENT SHOW.”
And Tae would perform for the very first time.

HORSE CITY'S GREATEST SHOW

Backstage, Tae waited for his turn.
He peaked out at the crowd.
There were hundreds of horses!
They were dancing and cheering.
The Canyon Stallions were performing
their hit country song.
The crowd went wild!
They were the most popular band in Horse City.

When their turn was over, they bowed and came backstage.
Spotting Tae, they started poking fun at him.
“Do you really think a weirdo like you should be here?”
The Canyon Stallions were always cruel to Tae the Tiger.
But, he didn’t listen to them.
Tae was about to perform.

Tae picked up his guitar and walked onstage.
The lights were bright and the crowd was in anticipation.
Tae sat down, took a deep breath and began to play.
His claws moved with skill and grace over the strings
He was plucking and strumming a fantastic tune.

Place the favorite greeting card you received here

· HOLIDAY NOTES ·

• HOLIDAY NOTES •

www.ingramcontent.com/pod-product-compliance
Lightning Source LLC
Chambersburg PA
CBHW081137300726
48982CB00006B/983

* 9 7 8 1 6 2 9 6 7 2 6 5 6 *